superjuice for kids

superjuice
for kids

michael van straten

mitchell beazley

Superjuice for Kids

Michael van Straten

First published in Great Britain in 2006 by Mitchell Beazley,
an imprint of Octopus Publishing Group Limited, 2–4 Heron
Quays, London E14 4JP.
© Octopus Publishing Group Limited 2006
Text © Michael van Straten 2006

A CIP catalogue record for this book is available from the
British Library.

ISBN 10: 1-845332-29-6
ISBN 13: 978-1-845332-29-7

While all reasonable care has been taken during the
preparation of this edition, neither the publisher, editors
or the author can accept responsibility for any consequences
arising from the use thereof or from the information
contained therein.

Commissioning Editor: Rebecca Spry
Executive Art Editors: Nicola Collings and Yasia Williams
Design: Geoff Borin
Editor: Jamie Ambrose
Proofreader: Vanessa Kendall
Photography: Francesca Yorke
Stylist: Fizz Collins
Production: Jane Rogers
Index: John Noble

Printed and bound by Toppan Printing Company in China
Typeset in Balance and Impact

contents

how food affects kids' health

Finally, the penny has dropped: parents who may have been concerned for years about the nutritional quality of the food their children are eating have now come face to face with some unpalatable truths.

It's twenty-five years since I made an hour-long radio documentary which I called *The Junk Food Generation*. I interviewed doctors, teachers, psychologists, criminologists, nutritionists, many parents, and even more children in America and the UK. The overall impression was one of impending disaster, as the experts had already identified evidence of links between food and function.

Of course, everyone knows that missing out on iron can cause anaemia, not enough vitamin C can give you scurvy, and the bone-deforming childhood disease rickets is the result of too little calcium and not enough vitamin D. But what was emerging from America were the results of studies linking nutritional deficiencies and excessive consumption of refined carbohydrates and artificial additives to learning difficulties, behavioural problems, and even criminal activity.

The great pioneer who first demonstrated the link between food additives and Attention Deficit Hyperactive Disorder (ADHD) was American allergist Dr. Ben Feingold. When I brought him to England in the early 1970s to give a public lecture, hundreds of desperate parents turned up, plus quite a few teachers – but virtually no doctors.

Thirty years later, what has changed?

Unfortunately there are still some academics who maintain that dyslexia doesn't exist, that ADHD is merely the result of bad parenting and poor discipline, and that there is no link between junk food, under-achievement, and behavioural problems.

Recently, the focus of attention on the appalling quality of food served up to the nation's children and young people in schools has been extraordinary. At last the urgency of these messages is beginning to hit home. More and more young children are developing type-2 diabetes, which should be a disease of middle age, and we're finding teenagers with damage to the walls of their arteries associated with an enormous increase in the risk of heart disease. There is a rising tide of obesity and there are ever-decreasing levels of physical activity. Many grandparents are now more active than their grandchildren. The chances of parents outliving their children are greater than they've been since the early 1900s. To me, that's horrifying.

big business and food

What makes matters worse are the battalions of big businesses – manufacturers of confectionery, snacks, crisps, and drinks – who are peddling high-sugar, high-fat, high-salt products containing every allowable colouring, flavouring, preserving, and sweetening chemical to our kids.

But that's only one side of the coin.

Big businesses work hard to use their influence behind the scenes to try to affect the policies of government, local authorities and individual schools. They use back-door promotions cloaked in the "feel-good" disguise to reward sport or scholastic achievement; all the kids have to do is buy more of their health-destroying products to have a chance of getting the prizes.

In some American states, where education authorities have tried to ban the ubiquitous canned drinks from vending machines and replace them with water or pure juices, giant corporations have threatened legal action to protect their commercial interests. Cash-strapped schools and hospitals allow fast-food outlets and burger vans onto their premises just to make money. What messages do these public endorsements of health-destroying foods give to our impressionable young people?

Yet the sin of including large amounts of some of the worst food ingredients is only one half of this appalling story. The other half is the sin of omission. Not only do most of these junk foods contain little, if any, of the vital fresh fruit and vegetables that we all need, but their very presence and easy availability pushes the right foods out of the diets of our children, who need them more than anyone.

Sure, big businesses have gone to extraordinary lengths to persuade children to eat vegetables – but it's processed vegetables. We've seen chocolate-flavoured Brussels sprouts, cartoon cut-out carrots, and every variety of crisp, chip, and potato snack. Sadly, it's often the high-fat, high-salt crisps and chips that still win

how to change habits

Before almost every home had a microwave, a freezer, and a supermarket on the doorstep; in an age when there wasn't a take-away or an endless selection of junk food close by; in the good old days when the only "fast food" was fish and chips, children ate what they were given. That included fresh fruit and vegetables.

Now, despite all the publicity about school meals, the government's five-portions-a-day campaign, and a stream of articles and news stories about healthy eating, many young people still don't eat enough fruit and vegetables. Yet these foods make a vital contribution to immediate good health, growth, and natural resistance and they're also a key factor in the long-term prevention of heart disease, premature ageing, and many forms of cancer.

Of course, it's largely your choice what babies eat. When they're teenagers, you can try logic and persuasion to steer them towards healthy choices. It's the toddlers to ten-year-olds who can be a problem. But there are ways.

My wife uses a cunning trick when she gives juice demonstrations to children at our local play scheme. Those who love fruit milk shakes or smoothies are quite happy to take the drink and get on with whatever activity they're involved in. She gets the reluctant ones to pour the milk into the blender, add the fruit (which they invariably say they don't like), then press the button. Presented with something they've made themselves, they're far less likely to say: "Yuk! I don't like that." When she cajoled a five-year-old into making his own strawberry milk shake at a smaller demonstration, his mother admitted afterwards that it was the first time her son had ever chosen to eat fruit. So the message is: get them involved.

There is one sure-fire way to get youngsters to try different foods and learn to enjoy both the pleasures and health benefits of a healthy diet – simply get them involved in the process of preparing and/or cooking fruit and vegetables.

That's why I firmly believe that juicing can be the answer to every parent's prayer when it comes to making sure that the young ones get a sensible and balanced diet.

why and how to juice

Fruit and vegetables provide many of the vitamins, minerals, and complex carbohydrates youngsters need in order to grow, thrive, and develop. They also provide the protective antioxidants that help prevent heart disease, degenerative changes, and many forms of cancer.

Fresh fruit and vegetables should make up roughly a third of your child's or young person's total daily food. But with the best will in the world, getting them to eat what's good for them isn't always easy. The five-portions-a-day advice for fruit and vegetables is now widely publicized, but it's just as widely misunderstood. What is a portion? What counts and what doesn't? Will five glasses of orange juice do the trick?

The answer is simple. A portion is roughly the size of your fist: one apple, one pear, one peach, two plums, a dozen grapes, a couple of small carrots, six Brussels sprouts, one head of broccoli, one banana. It should all add up to about 700g (1lb 9oz) in weight, though obviously this figure would be proportionately less for a small child. Potatoes don't count, but you can score a glass of commercial juice (but not squash) as one portion.

Dried fruit counts. All salads and cooked vegetables count, too. Smoothies use the whole fruit, so they count the same as fresh produce. A glass of a smoothie such as Blackapple Booster (*see* page 24) in the morning, The Californian (page 74) at lunchtime, and Dried Delight (page 118) before bed, plus a couple of tomatoes and salad and a portion of peas, green beans, broccoli or any other vegetable, will make up your child's five daily portions.

If you want your family to be super-healthy, then take a tip from me: up that fresh produce intake from five to seven portions a day. With the recipes in this book, that won't be a problem and you'll be giving everyone in the family an even more certain guarantee of good health and maximum protection.

why juice for kids

As well as being simple, juicing can be inexpensive. Whether they're three or twenty-three, your children will get some of the enormous health benefits of nature's bounty from juices and juice-based drinks. In this *Superjuice* book there are juices, fruit spritzers, milk shakes, and smoothies to suit all tastes. Even children with a milk allergy or a lactose intolerance are catered for with some delicious alternatives.

As a naturopath, I've been recommending juicing to my patients for more than forty years. It was at their insistence that I wrote *Superjuice* in 1999. Happily, the idea of juicing appealed to a much wider audience than those with health problems looking for nutrition-based solutions. The book has become a worldwide bestseller and resulted in hundreds of emails and letters from parents and grandparents asking for a children's version.

Youngsters who would run a mile from a beetroot, a stick of celery, an avocado, a bunch of grapes, and, particularly, a portion of cabbage will lap up these drinks and ask for more. Every one of them provides some of the vitamins and minerals your child needs. Some contain protein, others protective enzymes, but what they all have in common is the presence of the elusive

phytochemicals: those magical, recently discovered, and uniquely important protective substances found naturally in plants. These provide the natural defences for every single cell in the body, and a lack of them is the inevitable consequence of a junk-food diet with a paucity of wonderful fresh fruit and vegetables.

As well as all-round health benefits, each juice has a specific therapeutic value and you can use these benefits to persuade youngsters to at least give them a try. For example, your twelve-year-old with flu who's desperate to play in the football competition next week would drink Berries and Bugs (see page 82) if you explain that it will speed his recovery. Fifteen-year-olds of either sex will drink Zit Zapper (page 91) every day to get rid of their spots, but you'd have no luck putting a bowl of apple, celery, carrot, beetroot, and parsley in front of them for lunch. When it comes to exams, the Brain Blend (see page 77) of tofu, soya milk, chocolate powder, maple syrup, and nutmeg will keep them up to the mark.

Eating habits are largely determined by very early food experiences. If you can avoid commercial baby foods as far as possible and start with home-made fruit and vegetable purées without added sugar and with absolutely no salt, your baby is much more likely to be a fresh fruit- and veg-eating toddler and to carry these preferences into adult life. The appropriate juices in this book can be diluted one-third juice to two-thirds water and are a much healthier alternative to most of the commercially available squashes, fruit syrups, and other baby drinks.

As your children get older, try to keep them away from canned fizzy drinks. These not only rot teeth, they can also weaken bones and are an enormous source of empty calories. Even worse, the sugar-free varieties are full of artificial sweeteners, which are of no benefit whatsoever to a small child and are potentially hazardous in excessive quantities. Instead, make your own Old English Lemonade (see page 67) or any of the other health-giving recipes you'll find on the following pages.

juicing kit

There are many types of juicers and I've tried most of them — at prices ranging from £20 to £500+. You have two basic choices.

The generally less expensive is a centrifugal juicer, which whizzes the fruit or vegetables round on a serrated blade, allowing the juice to strain through a filter. The pulp is either retained inside the machine or thrown out into a separate container. For two or three glasses it doesn't make much difference, but for larger amounts you'll have to stop and remove the pulp to clear the filter before you start again.

The second type is a masticating juicer, which crushes the produce between special rollers. These work at lower speeds and much more juice is extracted, leaving a very dry pulp that is automatically extruded by the machine. These tend to be the most expensive, larger, and heavy pieces of equipment, but they're no doubt the Rolls Royce of juicers if you're really serious. In my opinion, the best models are The Champion and The Green Machine.

The juicer I use every day is the SuperJuicer — in which I have absolutely no commercial interest. It's a centrifugal machine that throws out the pulp, has a high extraction rate, and, importantly, is easy to clean. (Note from my wife: the serrated blades from all centrifugal machines need to be rinsed off immediately.) It costs around £200; phone 0115 9608646 for details.

If you've never juiced before, start with an inexpensive machine. If juicing small quantities for children, you couldn't do better than The Easy Health Juicer, a hand machine that costs around £30. Phone 0845 4588177 for details.

energy

juices

Rich in: Vitamin C from the currants and berries; skin and muscle-protective enzymes from the pineapple; potassium from the banana.

Good for: Building resistance to infection; speeding recovery from injury (this also applies if your youngster is unfortunate enough to need surgery for any reason); beating cramp in competitive sports.

blue boost

Black and blue may remind your kids of the bruises they get falling off skateboards or bumping their heads in the rush to get out of school, but this juice will soon see them back on their feet and smiling. And there's the added natural sweetness of maple syrup to wipe away the tears.

blackcurrants 280g (10oz)
blueberries 280g (10oz)
pineapple a quarter
banana 1, peeled
maple syrup about 1 tbsp

Put the currants, berries, and pineapple through a juicer.

Put into a blender and add the banana.

Whizz until smooth.

Serve sweetened with just enough maple syrup to take away the tartness.

Rich in: Carbohydrates and potassium from the bananas; vitamin C and healing enzymes in the mango; natural sugars from the mango and honey; protein and natural plant chemicals in the soya milk.

Good for: Sustained and instant energy; protection against cramp; encouraging the healing of sports wounds; helping young women overcome the often difficult effects of premenstrual syndrome.

yes, we have bananas

And there are lots in this filling and sustaining juice. If your children or young adults don't fancy breakfast, this will give them a good, energy-filled start to the day. It's particularly useful if they need to boost their carbs in preparation for a day on any sort of sports field. Soya milk is great for anyone with an intolerance to dairy food – and in this juice you'll hardly notice the taste, which some people find peculiar.

bananas 3, peeled
mango 1, peeled, stone removed, and cubed
runny honey 1 tbsp
soya milk 1 mug

Put all the ingredients into a blender and whizz until smooth, adding more soya milk if necessary.

vital statistics

Rich in: Calcium from the yogurt; potassium from the banana; vitamin B from the brewer's yeast; natural sugar from the honey.

Good for: Building strong bones; relieving cramp during exercise (which is why top tennis players eat bananas between matches); protecting against high blood pressure, heart disease, and fluid retention. Yogurt can also protect against osteoporosis (particularly in young girls) as your kids get older.

banana-to-go-go

Most kids love bananas, and this is a way to entice them to eat other good things, too. Yogurt is great for building bones. Yeast is a good source of vitamin B. And honey makes this yummy for little ones, as it's the best of natural sugars. If you have teenage girls who are unnecessarily worried about their weight, tell them the truth: bananas *aren't* fattening; in fact, they contain only 100 calories – far fewer than a handful of chips.

natural live yogurt 100ml (about 4fl oz)

banana 1, peeled

brewer's yeast 2 tsp

runny honey 1 tsp

Put all the ingredients into a blender and whizz until smooth.

vital statistics

Rich in: Vitamin C, potassium, and fibre from all the fruit; betacarotene from the oranges; aromatic compounds from the grapes; bioflavonoids from the lemon.

Good for: Convalescing and giving extra energy after any illness; soothing gum complaints; building up protection against cancer; general good nourishment and strength.

grape vine

Most children love grapes, and this mixture of grapes, lemon, and oranges is bound to be a family favourite. Adding the sparkling mineral water gives it a party feel, which goes down well at any celebration and is far healthier than any of the commercially produced fizzy drinks.

grapes 8 large seedless, black or green

oranges 2

lemon a half

sparkling mineral water half a glass

Put the grapes through a juicer.

Squeeze the oranges and lemon by hand or with a citrus juicer.

Mix all the juices together.

Add to the mineral water and stir.

vital statistics

Rich in: Vitamin C; vitamin A; betacarotene; the digestive enzyme papain.

Good for: Any young person whose digestion is interfering with energy levels; children with skin problems; any dysfunction of the mucus membranes, such as sinus infection or chronic catarrh.

hello, papa

Pawpaws or papayas are the most wonderful fruit, and are now available in the UK all year round. They lend themselves to fabulous juices mixed with other fruit, but this one gives the pawpaw its ultimate glory – served on its own.

pawpaw 2

Just juice them and add water if you want a lighter texture.

vital statistics

Rich in: Masses of vitamin C and fibre from the fresh fruit; extra easily absorbed fibre from the apricots; calcium from the milk.

Good for: Any energetic sportsperson, particularly if prone to or recovering from any infection or viral illness such as flu; young people with that irritating tendency to acne; those with digestive problems, particularly constipation; young women wanting to protect themselves from osteoporosis in later life.

blackapple booster

Why do people disregard blackberries? They're easily available in any country hedgerow and in many inner-city parks these days. And they're free. Add the apple, kiwi fruit, the delicious natural sweetness of dried apricots, and a mug of milk and your kids will have the most wonderful milk shake going.

blackberries 150g (5½oz)
red apple 1
kiwi fruit 2
dried apricots 6, ready-to-eat
full-fat milk 1 mug

Put the blackberries, apple, and kiwi fruit through a juicer.

Pour into a blender with the apricots and milk.

Whizz until smooth, adding more milk if necessary.

vital statistics

Rich in: Vitamin C, fibre, and cancer-fighting antioxidants from the cranberries.

Good for: Maintaining general energy levels; avoiding constipation; cleansing the skin; treating cystitis and other urinary infections.

apple berry

Cranberries shouldn't be left for Christmas – or, if you have American blood, Thanksgiving. They're delightful all year round and available fresh, if you're lucky, or frozen in most supermarkets. Here, they're combined with other kids' healthy favourites: apples and pears. The ingredients may sound slightly sour, but they're wonderfully sweet when served together.

apples 2
pear 1
cranberries 85g (3oz), fresh or defrosted frozen
grapes 8 large seedless, black or green
lime 1

Put the first four ingredients through a juicer.

Get the juice from the lime by squeezing or using a citrus juicer.

Mix well to serve.

vital statistics

Rich in: Vitamin A from the carrots, which also give some protection against ultraviolet radiation; potassium and soluble fibre from the pears; essential oils and vitamins A and C from the parsley.

Good for: Treating diarrhoea; relieving dry and scaly skin; helping protect against sunburn (but only as an add-on effect to the use of high-SPF sunscreens); ensuring your kids have enough fibre, as well as energy in abundance.

a great pair

Even kids who don't like carrots served as vegetables will like this. Juiced carrots, like many other juiced vegetables, take on a sweetness you don't find when they're cooked. This juice tastes like a slightly robust orange juice with the sweetness of pears, and has the added nutritional benefit of the parsley.

carrots 6
pears 2
parsley small handful

Feed the carrots and pears through the juicer, interspersed with the parsley.

Rich in: Vitamin C and fibre from all the ingredients; betacarotene from the carrots.

Good for: Any child suffering fatigue which is zapping energy and is due to mild anaemia or other blood disorders; digestive problems that interfere with the absorption of nutrients.

let's beet 'em

Sending your kids out to the footie field, tennis court, a swimming marathon or the Pony Club games? This is just what they need: a win-them-all mixture of the best natural ingredients. When they come home with the medal, cup or rosette, they'll know who's the real winner: the mum or dad who sent them off in the morning with a glass of this delicious juice.

beetroot 1 large, with 2 large leaves
carrots 2
apple 1 large

Put all the ingredients through a juicer.

Mix well before serving to your winning kid.

Rich in: Calcium from the milk; protein in the peanut butter; more calcium from the ice-cream; heart-friendly mono-unsaturated fatty acid from the peanuts.

Good for: Instant energy; bone protection; heart protection – yes, even your children need it.

peanut butter special

Tell them this ice-cream and peanut butter sundae will do them good and they'll never believe you. But it does. It's full of energy and bone protection, with natural sweetness from the maple syrup. A great beverage to serve up when they come home with that winning medal.

full-fat milk 1 mug
peanut butter 1 tbsp, smooth
vanilla ice-cream 1 scoop
maple syrup about 1 tbsp

Put the milk and peanut butter into a blender and whizz until smooth.

Pour into a tall glass and serve with the ice-cream and maple syrup on top.

immune

juices

vital statistics

Rich in: Vitamin C and soluble fibre (which helps the body get rid of toxins), from the strawberries; essential fatty acids – also from the strawberries – the vital building blocks of every body cell, particularly those in the brain and central nervous system; more vitamin C from the raspberries; calcium from the yogurt, to help build strong bones.

Good for: Any child who has digestive problems and needs to get rid of toxins; children who have short-term stomach upsets or diarrhoea (but if they continue for more than twenty-four hours, especially in very young children, get them to the doctor immediately).

berry nice

No child – or adult, for that matter – could fail to be impressed by this brilliant mixture of strawberries, raspberries, yogurt, and orange juice. It is, of course, best if you can use fresh fruit and home-made freshly squeezed orange juice, but frozen fruit is fine when it's out of season. Strawberries get a bit mushy when they're frozen, but they're still good for blending.

strawberries 5 large
raspberries 10
natural live yogurt 4 tbsp
oranges 1–2, depending on size

Juice the strawberries and raspberries.

Put them into a blender with the yogurt and whizz until smooth.

Juice or squeeze the oranges and use the juice to dilute to the required consistency.

vital statistics

Rich in: Vitamin C and soluble fibre from the fruit; calcium from the yogurt; easily digested protein from the whey powder.

Good for: Any child or young person who's getting over any sort of illness and who needs that extra boost to get back on top form.

very berry

Delicious at any time of year, this fruity smoothie will be a firm favourite with anyone recovering from an illness and waiting to get his or her appetite back. It's the perfect breakfast drink: either thick and eaten with a spoon or diluted and drunk from a glass or mug.

summer fruit 225g (8oz), such as strawberries, raspberries, red-, black- or whitecurrants or any others available. In winter you can use frozen defrosted berries and currants

natural live yogurt 150ml (5fl oz)

whey protein powder 1 tbsp (from any health-food store and most chemists)

Put the fruit through a juicer.

Pour into a blender with the yogurt and whey powder and whizz until smooth.

Dilute to the required consistency with cold water.

vital statistics

Rich in: Bromelain from the pineapple, which attacks only dead and damaged tissue and doesn't irritate the digestive tract; calming digestive agents in the mint; vitamin C and soluble fibre from the carrots.

Good for: Any child or young person recovering from surgery or the normal cuts and bruises of childhood; those suffering from stomach problems, especially constipation.

minty pineapple

Although it's normally classified as an "exotic" fruit, pineapple is now available all year round in practically every supermarket, and certainly in most Indian, African, and Asian shops. That's good news, because pineapples contain very useful enzymes which are essential for rebuilding skin tissue.

pineapple half a medium
mint 1 large sprig
carrots 4 large

Cut the pineapple into slices (no need to peel).

Put all three ingredients through a juicer.

Mix well before serving.

vital statistics

Rich in: Vitamin C and soluble fibre from the raspberries; more vitamin C from the pink grapefruit (which is richer in this vitamin than the white variety) and which also contains potassium.

Good for: Relieving mouth infections (thank the raspberries for that); sore throats and bleeding gums (the gifts from the grapefruit).

barbie bright

The fabulous blend of bright-red raspberries and the subtle pink of the grapefruit will make this any young girl's Barbie favourite. And it's full of goodness, too, thanks to the amazing nutrients in these wonderful fruits.

raspberries 1 small punnet – about 200g (7oz)
pink grapefruit a half

Put the raspberries through a juicer.

Juice or squeeze the grapefruit.

Mix the two juices together.

vital statistics

Rich in: Vitamin C from the oranges and limes; potassium, zinc, iron, folic acid, and calcium from the banana; much more calcium from the milk and yogurt; vitamin B-complex and vitamin E from the wheatgerm.

Good for: Any child or young person recovering from an infectious, bacterial or viral illness, such as coughs, colds or flu; building up zinc reserves from the banana, which help with the absorption of vitamin C, essential for anyone wanting extra immunity; children needing extra help in combating stress while they get themselves back on their feet.

lime-e-shake

This fab smoothie combines the wonderful flavour of citrus fruits with the smoothness of banana, milk, and yogurt. With all these delicious taste-bud burners, they'll hardly notice the addition of wheatgerm – which, if I'm truthful, isn't the most palatable of grains.

oranges 2
lime 1
banana 1
milk 300ml (10fl oz)
natural live yogurt 150ml (5fl oz)
wheatgerm 2 heaped tbsp

Squeeze the oranges and lime or put into a citrus juicer.

Put the orange and lime juice into a blender with the rest of the ingredients.

Whizz until smooth.

vital statistics

Rich in: Vitamin C from the kiwi fruit; refreshing, very low-calorie water content from the cucumber.

Good for: A high-kick boost of restorative vitamin C for anyone getting over an illness; a gentle laxative effect from the kiwi fruit.

cute kiwi

Thank goodness kiwi fruit have now outlasted their fashionable image as just a trendy garnish and can be seen as the nutritious fruits they really are. Weight for weight, they contain almost twice as much vitamin C as oranges and more fibre than apples. Yes, their furry skins may be a bit off-putting for kids, but in this juice you don't have to worry about the hairy bits as the juicer gets rid of them all. A wonderful grass-green colour, this drink is health in a glass.

kiwi fruit 3
cucumber 1 medium, unpeeled

Put both ingredients through a juicer. Mix well to serve.

vital statistics

Rich in: Cancer- and cholesterol-fighting chemicals from the spring onion; vitamins A and C in the pepper; more vitamin C and essential oils from the parsley; an extra boost of vitamin C and cancer-protective lycopene from the tomatoes.

Good for: Sore throats, coughs, and catarrh; any child who's getting over flu or suffering from an ongoing debilitating illness, such as ME; any child who has just come out of hospital after surgery (look also for any of the juices containing pineapple, which contains specific enzymes that help to heal scars).

spring thyme

This is a power-pack of nutrients. Tell your kids what it contains and they're likely to say, "Yeah, yeah." Give them a glass of it, or better still, get them to make it themselves, and they'll say, "That's cool."

spring onion 1

thyme 1 large sprig, leaves stripped off the stalks

green pepper a half, stem and core removed

cucumber a half

parsley 2 sprigs

tomatoes 4

lemon 1 wedge

Put all the ingredients, apart from the lemon, through a juicer.

Squeeze the lemon into the juice and mix well before stirring.

vital statistics

Rich in: Digestive essential oils from the mint; tons of vitamin C from the fruit – in fact, a quarter of a day's fresh fruit and veg "5-a-day" servings for one child from the oranges; a sparkly tingle from the mineral water.

Good for: Getting the kids ready for the first term at school (or back at school) when they might be vulnerable to a whole lot of bugs they didn't get at home; any "poorly tummy" complaints that they might have; any young people who say they don't want any drink unless it's fizzy.

fizzy oj ok

Straight orange juice may be a bit boring for little ones, but add the fizz of sparkling water and they'll love it. This has a tiny bit of mint, too, which gives it a slight – but not too strong – herbal flavour.

mint 3 large leaves
oranges 2
sparkling mineral water
about half a glass

Put the mint leaves over the conical part of a citrus juicer.

Juice the oranges through them.

Dilute with the mineral water.

Rich in: Cynarine from the artichokes, which helps digest fats; anti-cancer agents in garlic; potassium and sulphur from the radishes; vitamin C and soluble fibre from the carrots and apples.

Good for: Any young person with digestive problems; young women with fluid retention and bloating when starting their periods; any child unfortunate enough to show early indications of gout, arthritis, rheumatism or raised cholesterol levels (these should be checked by a specialized paediatrician as early as possible and any dietary changes made only after consultation).

jerusalem juice

Look at the funny, knobbly Jerusalem artichoke and you'll wonder how it ever evolved. These vegetables (which were, in fact, first grown in North America – nothing to do with the Middle East) have a sweetly peppery taste, which sophisticated young palates will love. Just in case your kids are not so sure, I've added the sweetness of carrots and apples, too.

jerusalem artichokes 2
garlic 1 clove, peeled if the skin is tough
radishes 2
carrots 4
apple 1

Put all the ingredients through a juicer. Mix well before serving.

Rich in: Mega-cancer-fighting lycopene from the tomatoes; vitamin C from the chilli; potassium, calcium, sulphur, vitamin C, folic acid, and selenium from the radishes.

Good for: A great boost of vitamin C when the kids are feeling low: building up protection against cancer for when they're older; stimulating spices in the Tabasco.

hot & sweet

Like a runny type of sauce on top of their favourite (organic, I hope) burger, this juice will be a favourite for the spicy kids in your household. It's strong, robust, and boasts a definite kick from the chilli, mustard, cress, radishes, and Tabasco.

tomatoes 2
green pepper 1, **stem and cores removed**
mild sweet chilli 1, **stem and seeds removed**
radishes 3, **with tender leaves**
tabasco a dash (optional)
mixed mustard and cress a handful

Put the tomatoes, pepper, chilli, and radishes through a juicer.

Stir in the Tabasco and mix thoroughly.

Serve with the mustard and cress scattered on top.

sports

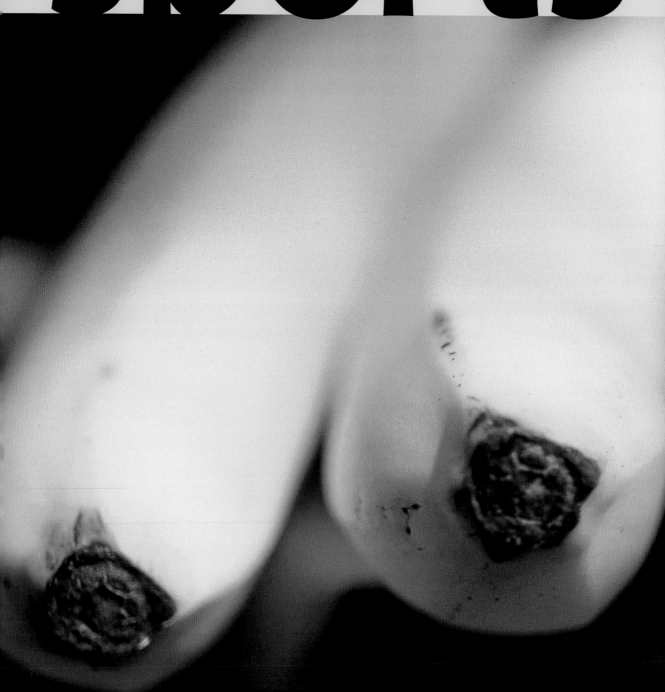

juices

Rich in: Essential oil from the ginger; natural enzymes and energy from the mango and pineapple; ample vitamin A from the betacarotene in the mango – important for skin, eyesight, and resistance.

Good for: Any young athlete heading for a tournament and thinking he or she is starting to get a cold; relief from bruising after the big match; building up energy if your kids are budding Beckhams or looking to take over from Venus Williams.

hot & tropical

Any child or young person who likes Chinese food will appreciate the eastern flavour of this juice. The tanginess of ginger combines so well with the sweetness of mango and pineapple.

root ginger 1cm ($1/2$-inch) piece, **peeled and finely chopped**
pineapple a half
mango a half, stone removed

Put all the ingredients through a juicer and mix well before serving.

Rich in: Digestive essential oils zingiberene and gingerols in the ginger; vitamin C from the kiwi fruit; bruise-relieving properties in the bromelain enzyme in the pineapple.

Good for: Any child who's passionate about a contact sport – such as rugby or boxing – or a sport that involves him or her taking an occasional tumble. Ideal if anxiety causes nausea.

ginger them up

Ginger may not seem the most likely spice to give to kids or young people, but it's a wonderful digestive and wards off all types of coughs, colds, and nausea – important if they're due on the track or field or in the pool the next morning. It's also good for their younger siblings, who may be prone to motion sickness as they're travelling with you to cheer on their brothers and sisters.

root ginger 1cm (1/2-inch) piece, peeled and finely chopped

pineapple a quarter

mint half a handful

kiwi fruit 2

Put all the ingredients through a juicer, interspersing the mint evenly.

Stir well to serve.

Rich in: Vitamin C and bioflavonoids from the cherries; natural energy-providing sugar, also from the cherries; extra vitamin C from the redcurrants, and even more from the apples, which are also a good source of the soluble fibre that can help relieve constipation or diarrhoea – a bane for any athlete.

Good for: Any sporty child who needs extra get-up-and-go, as well as vitamin C; relief from digestive complaints; increased resistance to infection.

cherry ripe

Cherry juice must be one of the prettiest of all. Yes, it is a bit of a bore stoning them, but it really is worth it – or you can buy frozen stoned cherries at most supermarkets these days. Redcurrants give extra colour, and adding the apple gives this juice a bite which is calmed down by the mineral water.

cherries 3 handfuls, stones removed
redcurrants a handful
apples 2
sparkling mineral water
125ml (4fl oz)

Put the fruit through a juicer.
Stir well into the mineral water.

Rich in: Vitamin C from all of the fruit, particularly the orange; extra betacarotene in the peach; the healing enzyme papain from the pawpaw; hydrating fluids from the mineral water.

Good for: All-round energy and protection for anyone – not just your Olympic potentials. You might need it yourself if you're driving them around most weekends trying to keep them in the frame.

pawpaw power

This mega-dose of nutrients is exactly what kids need to keep them up and running – or swimming, jumping, kicking or hitting – during their competitive season or in the run-up to the school games. You won't need to tempt them to try it; this looks and tastes like a gold medal in a glass.

pawpaw 1
peach 1, **stone removed**
orange 1
mineral water

Put the pawpaw and peach through a juicer.

Squeeze the orange or extract the juice using a citrus juicer.

Mix the two juices and add as much mineral water as you need to get the required texture – normally about half and half with the juice.

vital statistics

Rich in: Vitamin C and potassium, natural fructose and some betacarotene.

Good for: Rehydration before, during, and after the competition; extra energy and mineral replacement.

melon mélange

So refreshing and cooling, this is a great juice to give youngsters when they're going onto the sports field. Full of hydrating fluids and vitamin C, it will stop them craving fizzy, sugary drinks throughout whichever match they're playing.

cantaloupe melon 1
watermelon a half
honeydew melon a half

Put all the melons through a juicer.

Mix well to serve.

Rich in: Soluble fibre, vitamins A, C, and E, plus potassium from the pears; rehydrating water in the cucumber; huge amounts of betacarotene from the carrots.

Good for: Sustained energy; skin repair and protection; clear skin and efficient bowel function; good vision, especially in poor light conditions.

pear pressure

Light and refreshing, yet filling too, this juice is a wonderful combination of hydrating and energy-boosting nutrients. It also has great kid-appeal, thanks to its wonderful colour and natural sweetness. Yes, carrots do taste sweet when they're put through a juicer.

pears 2
cucumber half a medium
carrot 1 large

Juice all the ingredients.
Mix well before serving.

Rich in: Vitamin C from the lemons; antiviral and anti-bacterial phytochemicals from the elderflowers.

Good for: All youngsters who like to lead an active life – but it's just as important for the couch potatoes who need a boost to their natural defences.

flower-power syrup

Elderflower bushes grow like weeds in country hedgerows and many inner-city and suburban parks. They do have a strange smell, I must admit, but if you look at the price of elderflower cordial in your local supermarket, you'd hardly believe they were so easily available. This syrup, which you can dilute to whatever strength you like, makes use of this cheap and nutritious natural ingredient.

brown caster sugar
160g (5-6oz)

mineral water
just over 600ml (20fl oz)

elderflower 5 large heads

lemon 2 large, juiced

Put the sugar into a pan and pour in the water.

Bring to a simmer, stirring continuously, until the sugar has dissolved.

Add the elderflowers, flower heads down, and continue simmering for about seven minutes.

Pour in the lemon juice and leave until cold.

Strain and bottle. Dilute as required.

vital statistics

Rich in: Vitamin C from the orange, pineapple, and strawberries; injury-relieving enzymes in the pineapple; bone-protective calcium in the yogurt; cramp-preventing potassium from the banana, plus vitamin B$_6$ for period problems in the older girls; mega protein in the peanut butter.

Good for: All-round energy; immunity protection; building up bone mass.

muscle power

Smoothies are a great way to get extra nutrition into your kids. Tell them that this contains peanut butter and they'll go, "Wow!". As well as yummy peanut butter, however, this also has a mega-dose of other essential ingredients, which will help any young athlete reach his or her full potential.

orange 1
pineapple a half
strawberries 6 large
natural live yogurt small carton
banana 1
peanut butter 1 heaped tbsp, smooth

Squeeze the orange by hand or use a citrus juicer.

Juice the pineapple and strawberries.

Put them all together in a blender with the yogurt, banana, and peanut butter and whizz until smooth.

muscle saver

The worst – and very painful – thing that can happen to any budding sportsperson is to be attacked by cramp just at the crucial point in an important match or competition. The inclusion of tomatoes in this juice makes that far less likely.

sweet potato 1 small
carrots 4
celery stalks 2, with leaves
tomatoes 2
parsley a handful

Put all the ingredients through a juicer.

Mix well to serve.

vital statistics

Rich in: Calcium and immune-boosting probiotic bacteria from the yogurt; digestive essential oils in the mint.

Good for: Replacing protein, calcium, and sodium used during physical activity.

after-sport lassi

When youngsters come home after a day of physical activity, they need a smoothie that's comforting, relaxing, cooling, and healthy. This is the one. Without them even knowing it, this juice helps build their bones for a long and active sporty life.

natural live yogurt 150ml (5fl oz)
sea salt a pinch
iced water 150ml (5fl oz)
mint 1 tbsp chopped leaves, plus 2 leaves to serve

Put all the ingredients into a blender and whizz until smooth.

Serve with the reserved mint leaves floating on top.

memory

juices

Rich in: Highly protective phytochemicals from the kale and cabbage; brain-boosting essential oils in sage.

Good for: Making sure that concentration, memory, and mental function all perform at their optimal levels; boosting the immune system and preventing infection at all-important times.

red dawn

Bright-red and beautiful, this is a wonderful juice to give the kids or adolescents first thing in the morning – particularly if they're not that fond of breakfast. It will give them a great start to the day and keep their concentration going until lunchtime.

red pepper 1, **stems and cores removed**
red apples 2
tomato 1
red cabbage a quarter
kale 2 leaves
sage 4 leaves

Alternating the sage with the rest of the ingredients, put them all through a juicer.

Stir well before serving.

vital statistics

Rich in: An enormous amount of aromatic antioxidant compounds from the grapes; extra anti-fatigue properties, also from the grapes; water to help prevent dehydration, which may cause headaches and loss of concentration; specific natural chemicals and fruit sugars in the grapes, which nourish and feed individual brain cells.

Good for: Beating fatigue; soothing sore throats.

heard it on the grapevine

So simple, so fresh – this pink juice will set any youngster's taste buds fizzing. Just the thing to give them as they face a morning in the exam room.

black grapes 20 large seedless
sparkling mineral water

Put the grapes through a juicer.

Measure the juice and add the same amount of mineral water.

Rich in: Vitamin C from the apples and lemon; soluble fibre from the apples; rehydrating fluids from the mineral water.

Good for: Young people who suffer from digestive disorders that may affect their ability to concentrate; young women just starting their periods who have bloating difficulties, which could interfere with their concentration, too.

old english lemonade

Forget the sugary or artificial-sweetener-loaded, very expensive lemonades you find on supermarket shelves. This is far healthier and cheaper.

green apples 3 medium
lemon a half
sparkling mineral water

Juice the apples.

Squeeze the lemon or put through a citrus juicer.

Mix the juices with the mineral water to the required taste and consistency.

vital statistics

Rich in: Betacarotene from the sweet potato; essential oils in the mint; vitamin C and soluble fibre from the apples.

Good for: Stimulating brain function and a general sense of happiness; eye function and protection – essential for anyone spending their days reading or working with computers; concentration and alertness.

apple jack

Mint is probably the most common herb found in the UK – and it's one most children and young people will be familiar with as an accompaniment to roast lamb. It's amazingly easy to grow; in fact, once its roots are established the only problem is stopping it taking over the rest of the garden. Here it's combined with apples and a sweet potato in a feel-good juice from which we could all benefit.

mint 6 large leaves
apples 2
sweet potato 1

Put all the ingredients through a juicer, alternating the mint with the apples and sweet potato.

Stir thoroughly before serving.

vital statistics

Rich in: Brain-protective essential fatty acids from the flaxseeds and strawberries; sustaining calcium and protein from the yogurt; protective vitamin C from all the fruit.

Good for: Any brain function; general all-round nutrition from the huge input of fibre and vitamin C from the fruit.

exam special

The GCSEs or A-levels are coming up. You've got teenagers getting into a strop, because they haven't done their coursework or revision. You end up on the morning of the exams and they're in a total panic. Give them this juice every morning for at least the month before they put pen to paper and you'll be doing your bit towards their A* grades.

peach 1, **stone removed**
apricots 2, **stones removed**
strawberries 6
natural live yogurt small tub
flaxseeds 1 tsp, ground

Put the peach, apricots and strawberries, through a juicer.

Put into a blender with the yogurt and whizz until smooth.

Serve with the flaxseeds sprinkled on top.

Rich in: Phytoestrogens and fenchone from the fennel; some potassium and sodium from the celery; soluble fibre and vitamin C from the apple and pear.

Good for: Reducing fluid retention and therefore improving blood flow to the brain; cerebral stimulation from the volatile oils in the fennel; relieving bloating in girls just before their periods, which can affect concentration.

mind & body

Although they're widely available, Florence fennel bulbs are a sadly neglected salad vegetable in the UK. However, they're an excellent addition to any salad and give it a crunchy, aniseed-like flavour. It's a wonderful vegetable to juice and, added to apples and celery, makes a peppery concoction that will appeal particularly to children and teenagers who don't have a sweet tooth.

fennel 1 small
celery stalks 2, with leaves
apple 1
pear 1

Put all the ingredients through a juicer. Stir well before serving.

vital statistics

Rich in: Phytoestrogens from the fennel; vitamin C and soluble fibre in the apple; tons more vitamin C, plus antibiotic oils and cancer-fighting chemicals from the watercress; cleansing, antiseptic, hormone-balancing and brain- and memory-enhancing properties from the sage.

Good for: Anyone who has to use their brain for work or study; short-term memory; concentration; cognitive function; and mental stamina.

fennel fancy

Bulb, or Florence, fennel is a delicious vegetable served steamed or roasted; as well as crunchy addition to any salad, and (in this case) a fabulous, aniseed-tasting juicing ingredient. It goes brilliantly with the combination of apple and watercress, and sage helps make this a super-nutrient juice.

fennel half a bulb
cooking apple 1 large
watercress 1 bunch
sage 1 sprig

Put all the ingredients through a juicer, alternating the sage with the fennel, apple, and watercress.

Mix well before serving.

vital statistics

Rich in: Vitamin B_6 from the banana; cancer-fighting and anti-ageing nutrients from the prunes; bone-enhancing properties in the soya or rice milk.

Good for: Sustained mental effort for exams, lectures or those first important job interviews.

the californian

Of all the dried fruits, prunes are the most amazing and the most underrated. They're excellent as a natural sweetener and will provide substantial amounts of essential nutrients. The banana will contribute some instant and slow-release energy.

californian prunes
6 large, pitted and ready-to-eat
banana 1
soya or rice milk 225ml (8fl oz)

Put all the ingredients into a blender and whizz until smooth.

vital statistics

Rich in: Betacarotene, vitamins, and fibre from the beetroot and carrots; the volatile oils linalool, limonene, and estragol in the basil.

Good for: Any child or teenager who gets exam nerves which result in stomach problems; also those whose classroom stress makes itself known in an outbreak of acne and other skin conditions.

flippin' brilliant

This one really is a sustaining brain juice. It's easy to make, colourful, and smells good, too. A great juice to start off a tiring day in the classroom.

beetroot 2
carrots 3
basil 2 large leaves

Put all the ingredients through a juicer, alternating the basil leaves with the beetroot and carrots.

Mix well to serve.

Rich in: Isoflavones from the tofu and soya milk; iron in the chocolate powder; instant energy from the maple syrup; the natural feel-good chemical myristicin in the nutmeg.

Good for: Settling raging hormones (in both boys and girls); blood nourishment; energy-boosting; mood-calming.

brain blend

Any good vegetarian will be aware of the health benefits of tofu as a replacement protein for meat. It doesn't have much flavour of its own, so here I've added chocolate powder, maple syrup, and nutmeg to give a delicious, slightly sweet and spiced juice.

tofu 2.5cm (1-inch) cube
soya milk 225ml (8fl oz)
chocolate powder 1 tsp good dark, such as Green & Black's
maple syrup 1 tsp
nutmeg 2 pinches

Put all the ingredients into a blender and whizz until smooth.

get-well

juices

vital statistics

Rich in: Vitamin C; cancer-fighting natural chemicals; natural chemicals which protect the whole gut.

Good for: General recuperation; building resistance to cancer; relieving and helping to prevent cystitis and other urinary infections – particularly important for young women.

cranberry crazy

It's one of God's great mistakes that cranberries don't grow well in the UK. Why did he reserve them just for North America? But you can buy them here around Thanksgiving and, of course, at Christmas. You'll also find them in many supermarkets' freezer cabinets. Failing that, use a good sugar-free cranberry juice. Kids love their bright, cherry-like colour.

fresh cranberries 350g (12oz)
(or use defrosted frozen fruit or a glass of unsweetened cranberry juice)
maple syrup 1 tsp

Juice the cranberries.

Sweeten with the maple syrup.

Rich in: Vitamin C and protective phytochemicals from the berries and cherries; gut-friendly and immune-boosting bacteria from the yogurt and Yakult.

Good for: Preventing the unwanted side-effects of antibiotics; speeding recovery from infection; a quick return to normal eating, strength, and vitality.

berries and bugs

All the berries, fresh or dried, are delicious and nutritious. They provide instant and slow-release energy. Combined here with millions of friendly bacteria, they're a terrific boost for any youngster's struggling immune system.

natural live yogurt 150ml (5fl oz)
yakult 1 pot
blueberries 3 tbsp
dried cherries 1 tbsp
dried apricots 4
ice a few cubes

Put all the ingredients into a blender and whizz until smooth.

vital statistics

Rich in: Cancer-fighting substances – cranberries are among the highest of the ORAC (Oxygen Radical Absorbence Capacity) foods; vitamin C; soluble fibre.

Good for: Easing digestive problems, particularly constipation; protecting against cystitis; boosting immunity.

apple supreme

This beautifully coloured juice will appeal to any child or teenager who says no to fresh fruit. It's full of goodness, looks great, and is simple to make. One glass will give them more than half of their daily needs of fresh produce. And it tastes delicious.

cranberries 275g (10oz), **fresh or defrosted frozen**
apples 2
orange 1

Put the cranberries and apples through a juicer.

Squeeze the orange or put through a citrus juicer.

Mix the juices together to serve.

vital statistics

Rich in: Vitamin C and betacarotene from the cabbage, kale, and broccoli (all members of the brassica family); more betacarotene from the carrots; vitamin C and soluble fibre from the apples and pear.

Good for: General immunity; relief of digestive problems; protection from cancer.

green dream

Yes, it is difficult to get some kids to eat greens, but this will astound them. It looks like a green, slimy mush – very appealing to naughty-minded under-tens – but is packed with nutrients. They won't know they're eating something healthy, but they'll love it. The apples, carrots, and pear give this juice a wonderful sweetness.

white cabbage a quarter
kale a small handful of leaves
broccoli 4 medium florets
apples 2
carrots 2
pear 1

Put all the ingredients through a juicer and mix well.

vital statistics

Rich in: Vitamin C from the strawberries, melon, and blueberries; calcium from the milk and organic ice-cream.

Good for: recovering from surgery or an illness. Encouraging youngsters with throat complaints to eat healthily, as the coolness of the ice-cream is very soothing; young girls, who need calcium to protect their bones as they grow older.

ice-cream milk shake

Yum, yum! That's what most kids will say to this great combination of healthy fruit, nutritious milk, and a big slug of delicious ice-cream. This is far better, both taste- and health-wise, than the commercially produced fruit ice-creams you find at your corner store or supermarket.

strawberries 6 large
cantaloupe melon a half
blueberries 2 tbsp
full-fat milk 1 glass
vanilla ice-cream 1 scoop

Put the strawberries, melon, and blueberries through a juicer.

Mix thoroughly with a fork.

Add the milk.

Top with the ice-cream to serve.

Rich in: The natural healing enzyme bromelain; antiviral essential oils in the cinnamon; feel-good myristicin from the nutmeg.

Good for: mood-enhancing, feel-good, and warming, this drink is good for any child who's feeling under the weather.

pineapple pick-me-up

The only way to judge the ripeness of a pineapple is by weight. If it feels heavy for its size, it will be full of sweet juice. The trick of pulling out the spiky leaves is meaningless. For this juice, only fresh will do, as all processed pineapple juices contain very little of the natural enzymes. Don't use boiling water for this juice as that, too, destroys the enzymes.

pineapple 1 small
hot water 300ml (10fl oz)
runny honey 1 tbsp
ground cinnamon 1 large pinch
ground nutmeg 1 large pinch

Juice the pineapple.

Put into a large mug and add freshly boiled water.

Stir in the honey and sprinkle with the spices.

Stir well to serve.

vital statistics

Rich in: Essential oils; vitamins A and C; iron; calcium; potassium; soluble fibre.

Good for: Building immunity and fighting infections; keeping skin healthy (important if your young person is going through a spotty stage); keeping constipation at bay and tackling other digestive problems.

zit zapper

It always seems strange to me that parsley is relegated to the edge of the plate as an almost obligatory garnish. It is an important herb, particularly for young girls, who may have water retention when they first start their periods. This juice is wonderfully colourful, thanks to the addition of beetroot, which is a sadly undervalued vegetable.

apple 1
celery 2 stalks
carrots 3
beetroot a half, with 2 leaves
parsley a small handful

Juice all the fruit and vegetables, adding the parsley gradually as you go.

vital statistics

Rich in: Carotenoids, folate, and potassium from the beetroot; iron, more folate, plus vitamin C from the cabbage and broccoli; extra soluble fibre from the apple.

Good for: Fatigue; ME; anaemia; recovery from infectious illnesses, such as glandular fever; constipation; boosting resistance.

beet it up

Even kids who don't like beetroot as a vegetable will be won over by this fresh-tasting, blood-red juice – which, in fact, is particularly good for any blood complaint. Beetroot has been used for centuries in central Europe to treat cancer, especially leukaemia. But it doesn't have to do you good to taste good. Just give a glass a day of this nutritious juice to your ailing child and see him or her thrive.

beetroot 2, with 4 leaves
red cabbage 2 leaves
broccoli 4 florets
apple 1

Put all the ingredients through a juicer. Mix well before serving.

vital statistics

Rich in: The essential oils gingerol and zingiberene from the ginger; volatile oils in the fennel; vitamin C from the grapes; other essential oils from the mint; more vitamin C and soluble fibre from the apples.

Good for: Children and young people with digestive problems, nausea, coughs, and colds. Particularly useful packed in a vacuum flask if you're travelling with youngsters prone to motion sickness.

tum tum

Ginger is quite a strong spice to give to children, but here its flavour is calmed by the addition of grapes and apples, most kids' favourite fruit. We also have fennel to give a slightly peppery flavour and lots of extra nutrients.

root ginger small fingernail-size piece, peeled and finely chopped
black grapes large handful seedless
fennel half a small bulb
mint half a handful
apples 2

Put all of the ingredients through a juicer.

Mix well to serve.

stress

juices

vital statistics

Rich in: Skin-protective silica from the cucumber and betacarotene from its skin; vitamin C and digestion-promoting enzymes in the pawpaw; the essential oil estragol from the tarragon.

Good for: Relieving skin problems, often a cause of stress in the young; maintaining a healthy digestion, which often suffers when youngsters are under pressure.

paw thing

The exotic pawpaw (or papaya) has a wonderfully soft texture and great soothing powers. Here, I've mixed it with cucumber and that useful herb tarragon, which is an aid to digestion.

cucumber 1 medium
pawpaw 1
tarragon 1 sprig

Juice all the ingredients.
Mix well before serving.

Rich in: Vitamins A, C, and E, plus fibre, from the mango; vitamin C, fibre, and betacarotene in the pawpaw; fibre and bromelain from the pineapple; vitamin C and betacarotene in the oranges; potassium, vitamin B_6, and folic acid from the banana.

Good for: General protection from coughs and colds; combating PMS in teenage girls; protection from cramp, thanks to the banana; stress-busting due to B_6 and potassium.

ace

What could be more appealing than this fabulous mixture of wonderful fruit containing the important protective A, C, and E vitamins? Tell your teenagers – particularly girls – that this is one of the best juices for giving them zit-free skin and they'll be hooked. The inside of mango or pawpaw skin, by the way, is a brilliant skin cleanser for girls who wear make-up.

oranges 2
lime 1
pawpaw a half
mango a half, stone removed
pineapple a quarter
banana 1

Put everything except the banana through a juicer.

Add to a blender with the banana and whizz until smooth.

Rich in: Calcium and friendly bacteria from the yogurt; masses of vitamin C; highly protective antioxidants in all the berries.

Good for: Strong bones in growing children; stress reduction, thanks to the extra calcium and B vitamins produced by the good bugs in yogurt; energy and vitality from the natural fruit sugars and protective chemicals.

flintstone fancy

Our ancient ancestors were cave-dwellers and they lived off the land. As hunter-gatherers, they ate little meat but lots of wild berries, nuts, roots, and seeds. This may seem very basic, but was enough to keep them strong and healthy – after all, they survived; the dinosaurs didn't.

blueberries, blackberries, cranberries, raspberries, strawberries 1 handful of each (or whatever similar fruit is available)
natural live yogurt 150ml (5fl oz)
runny honey 2 tsp

Place all the ingredients in a blender and whizz until smooth.

Rich in: Vitamin C and soluble fibre from both fruits; some potassium in the peaches.

Good for: Relieving digestive problems; providing an easily digestible source of good calories – useful if stress has put a youngster off his or her food; a quick boost to flagging blood-sugar levels.

pear & peach punch

These two favourite fruits combine well here to make a thick, delicious, naturally sweet juice which any child or young person will adore. The fact that it's doing them good won't even occur to them.

pears 2
peaches 2, **stones removed**

Juice the fruit.

Mix well before serving.

Rich in: Iodine from the watercress; vitamin C in the broccoli, spinach, and apples; folic acid from the spinach; fibre from all the ingredients.

Good for: Relieving all digestive complaints, especially constipation, which is often the result of stress and anxiety; high protective value against many types of cancer, thanks to phytochemicals in watercress, broccoli, and spinach.

granny's favourite

This wonderful collection of green fruits and vegetables makes a very attractive drink with a slightly peppery taste from the watercress. If your kids aren't great fans of vegetables, they'll love the added sweetness from the apples.

watercress a large handful
broccoli 3 large spears
spinach a handful
granny smith apples 2
pear 1

Put all the ingredients through a juicer. Mix well to serve.

Rich in: Vitamin C; volatile essential oils; bioflavonoids.

Good for: An immune boost and protects against colds and flu as well as other infectious diseases; stress and anxiety; insomnia.

super vit C

Citrus fruit don't seem very exotic, but they are so important for young people who, sadly, seldom bother to eat them. This spiced, hot fruit cup will appeal to all ages and supply loads of health-building vitamins and stress-easing natural ingredients.

orange 1
pink grapefruit 1
lime 1
cinnamon a pinch
nutmeg a pinch
runny honey 1 tsp

Squeeze the fruit, or use a citrus juicer.

Pour into a mug and top up with hot – not boiling – water, the spices, and the honey.

Mix well before serving.

vital statistics

Rich in: Sulphur from the cabbage; vitamin C and fibre in the apples and peppers; folic acid and potassium from the peppers; volatile oils in the basil.

Good for: Improving digestion; relieving skin complaints often associated with times of stress; general calming and stress relief.

green for blues

Basil isn't only one of the most delicious and versatile herbs, it also contains natural chemicals, which are known to have mildly sedative and mood-enhancing effects. Here, it shares its nutritional benefits with a cornucopia of other healthy food.

cabbage 4 large green leaves
apples 2
red pepper 1, stem and core removed
green pepper 1, stem and core removed
basil a scant half-handful of leaves

Interspersing the basil leaves with the other ingredients, put them all through a juicer.

Mix well before serving.

vital statistics

Rich in: Betacarotene, folate, potassium, iron, and vitamin C from the beetroot leaves; natural asparagines in the asparagus.

Good for: Recovering from a condition causing chronic fatigue; water retention immediately before a period.

beet & asparagus special

Just the look of this beautiful pink juice will be enough to set their taste buds singing. Even children and young people who don't like the flavour and texture of beetroot will be won over by the surprising sweetness it provides after juicing.

beetroot 2 medium, with leaves
asparagus 6 spears
sparkling mineral water

Put the beetroot and asparagus through a juicer.

Mix well and dilute with the mineral water to taste.

vital statistics

Rich in: Betacarotene from the carrots; the natural chemical asparagine in the asparagus.

Good for: Relief of urinary infections and constipation; reducing water retention, which makes it useful in those stressful days leading up to a young woman's period.

carrotgus

It may seem unusual to use a vegetable such as asparagus to make juice, but this great food treat works very well. It has been used for medicinal purposes for more than 500 years, and can particularly help young women when they first start their periods. What's more, it tastes great.

carrots 2 large
asparagus 6 spears
sparkling mineral water

Put the carrots and asparagus through a juicer.

Dilute the juice with the water to taste.

good-night

juices

Rich in: Essential oils from the ginger; soothing sweetness from the natural sugars in the honey; volatile warming oils from the cinnamon; relieving vitamin C from the lemon.

Good for: Any child feeling nauseous, whether it's after an upset stomach, recovery from any sort of surgery or just spending too long travelling in a car, plane or train; those suffering from throat complaints, congested sinuses or chesty coughs.

sweet snoozer

Here's a juice that is a gentle relief for anyone – children in particular – whose sleep patterns are disrupted by coughs, colds or bronchial problems. It's slightly sweet, thanks to the honey, so it won't taste like medicine despite its enormous nutritional benefits.

root ginger 1cm (half-inch) piece, peeled

runny honey 1 tbsp

cinnamon 1 pinch

lemon a quarter, plus a slice to serve

Grate the ginger into a saucepan and add a cup of water.

Bring to the boil, add the honey, and stir until dissolved.

Add the cinnamon, leave until warm, and strain.

Squeeze in the lemon just before serving and add a slice of lemon to float on the top of the drink.

Rich in: Masses of vitamin C; vital bioflavonoids; enzymes from the honey.

Good for: Soothing sore chests and throats; comforting fractious little ones by boosting low blood-sugar levels, which can make them irritable and prevent sleep.

rosehip syrup

Rosehip syrup is a traditional cure for colds, coughs, and flu, but it can be very sweet. This juice uses honey instead of sugar, which means that at least the sugars are natural. If you're lucky enough to have them in your garden, you'll get the rosehips for free during late summer and autumn.

water 1 mug
runny honey 1 tsp, runny
rosehips 85g (3oz), or 2 tsp of commercial rosehip syrup

Put all the ingredients into a saucepan and boil until the rosehips are soft.

Sieve, pushing the rosehips through the mesh to extract all the juice.

Dilute with extra water if necessary.

Rich in: A whole range of powerfully protective nutrients from the grapes; extra vitamin C and soluble fibre from the pears.

Good for: Children suffering from fatigue, anaemia, joint problems; little ones who are irritable due to low blood-sugar levels – a real problem in children who are difficult feeders.

up the grapes and pears

Yes, this is an alternative to the old Cockney rhyming slang of apples and pears, but it does just as well for little ones who need a nudge to get them up to their bedrooms. The nutritional values in both these easily available fruits will keep your children happy and comfy until it's time for playgroup or school in the morning.

green grapes 12 seedless
pears 2

Put the grapes and pears through a juicer.

Mix well before serving.

Rich in: Vitamin C from the lemon and apple; soluble fibre in the apple; warming, antiseptic, and anti-inflammatory substances from the ginger; cleansing properties from the water.

Good for: Sleeplessness caused by coughing, particularly related to bronchial infections; any child with digestive problems, such as constipation or diarrhoea – a common cause of sleep difficulties.

apple mack

Adults may think of ginger ale as an addition to whisky, but this light, fruity juice is great for kids. The ginger and lemon give it a zing, which contrasts with the soothing properties of the apple.

lemon a quarter
root ginger small fingernail-size piece, peeled
apple 1
sparkling mineral water half a glass

Squeeze the lemon.

Put the ginger and apple through a juicer.

Mix well with the lemon juice and dilute with the mineral water.

vital statistics

Rich in: Calcium from the milk; natural sugars in the honey; vitamin C and more natural sugars from the mango and strawberries; healing natural enzymes from the mango.

Good for: Any child who needs a soothing night-time drink; kids who need extra vitamins to get over colds or flu; chronic insomnia, which is often triggered by calcium deficiency.

good night, sweetheart

This delicious and naturally sweet juice will send your little darlings to bed happy. It's full of goodness and has the comforting properties of warm milk, which parents down the ages have known is a brilliant bedtime soother. Serve it with a kiss and a cuddle.

full-fat milk 1 mug
runny honey 1 tbsp
mango 1, stone removed
strawberries 6 large

Gently warm the milk and honey together until the honey is just dissolved. Don't let it boil or get too hot.

Juice the mango and strawberries.

Mix the two together and serve.

vital statistics

Rich in: Vitamin C and soluble fibre from the oranges and peach; carbohydrates and potassium from the banana; natural sugars from the honey.

Good for: Any child who gets cramp during the night; a kids who's off his or her food (they'll get good carbohydrates from the banana).

don't slip on this one

The days of jokes about slipping on banana skins may be over, but this juice is no joke. It's full of goodness and is bound to appeal to any child or young person needing a good night's sleep after a physically or mentally exhausting day.

oranges 2
runny honey 1 tbsp
banana 1
peach 1, stone removed

Squeeze the oranges or extract the juice with a citrus juicer.

Put into a blender with all the other ingredients.

Whizz until smooth.

vital statistics

Rich in: Betacarotene from the apricots; fructose in all the fruits; iron from the dates.

Good for: Faddy eaters who may be short of iron, so slightly anaemic; those with low blood-sugar levels, which can make them irritable and prevent sleep.

dried delight

Black grape juice does the same for your children's hearts and circulatory systems as a couple of glasses of red wine do for you: it's highly protective. But it also contains instantly absorbed fruit sugars, which are very calming. The vitamins and minerals in the dried fruit, together with their own natural sugars, make this the ideal bedtime drink for the over-tired and irritable youngster.

black seedless grapes 24 seedless, or 1 small glass of black grape juice

dried apricots 2, ready-to-eat

medjool dates 2, stones removed

lime-blossom honey 2 tsp

Put the grapes through a juicer.

Put the juice into a blender with the apricots, dates, and honey and whizz until smooth.

vital statistics

Rich in: Chlorophyll and folic acid from the spinach; high water content from the cucumber; betacarotene and fibre from the carrots; potassium from the lettuce.

Good for: Any child who can't get to sleep and who needs a boost of fibre from the carrots to ease their bowels; mild insomnia, as the lettuce supplies tiny traces of morphine-like chemicals.

popeye's punch

Spinach may not be most kids' favourite vegetable, but put through a juicer with the rest of these ingredients, it's a slightly sweet, (because of the carrots) relaxant to keep them calm through the night.

spinach a handful
cucumber a half
carrots 4
cos lettuce a quarter

Put all of the ingredients through a juicer.

Mix well to serve.

Rich in: Digestive enzymes from the mint; soluble fibre from the apples; masses of vitamin C from the kiwi fruit, plus potassium to help relieve night cramps.

Good for: Any child who may have been diagnosed as having irritable bowel syndrome (but your paediatrician must have confirmed that diagnosis); all children with colic, heartburn or indigestion; a teenager going through that spotty stage causing irritation that keeps them awake.

green clean

This is yet another green juice that's full of goodness, with wonderful cleansing and digestive properties that will help your children sleep the whole night through. It also contains soluble fibre, from the apples, which regulates bowel function.

mint 5 large leaves
apples 2
kiwi fruit 3

Roll up the mint leaves and feed into the juicer alternately with the apples and kiwi fruit.

Stir well before serving.

Rich in: Betacarotene from the carrots; vitamin C and soluble fibre from the apple; protein, antioxidants and plant hormones from the soya milk.

Good for: Kids whose sleep patterns are disrupted by digestion or bowel complaints; young girls whose hormone changes are beginning to be sleep-disruptive; those who need extra protein from soya to give them energy for the next day.

and soya to bed

There's a very wide misconception that many children are allergic to dairy products. But some of them really are – there's no doubt of that – and substituting soya milk is a good way of giving them the extra nutrients they won't get if they can't eat dairy produce. This juice gives them lots of vitamin C and fibre: a soothing mixture at bedtime.

carrots 2
apple 1
soya milk amount equal to the juice

Juice the carrots and apple.

Measure the amount of juice and add an equal quantity of soya milk.

Mix well before serving.

Rich in: Betacarotene from the carrots; vitamin C and soluble fibre in the apples; mildly soporific natural chemicals from the nutmeg; extra nutrients from the rice milk without the mucous-forming problems of cow's milk.

Good for: Any child or young person who has trouble getting to sleep; those with adverse reactions, allergy or lactose intolerance to milk; those who have any sort of digestive problem.

slumbertime

Nutmeg has a long and interesting history, dating back to the sixth century, when it was an important part of the spice trade and widely used in India and the Middle East. Victorian nannies in the UK caught on to its beneficial properties by adding it to rice puddings served as tea for their charges – thereby ensuring the little ones would go to sleep early and leave them with free evenings. In this juice, it's combined with carrots and apples and all their extra soothing nutrients.

carrots 2
apples 2
rice milk 1 mug
nutmeg 2 pinches

Put the carrots and apples through a juicer.

Add the rice milk.

Mix well and stir in the nutmeg.

raw ingredients a-z

Apples	Carotenes, ellagic acid, pectin, potassium, vitamin C
Apricots	Beta-carotene, iron, potassium, soluble fibre
Artichokes, Jerusalem	Inulin, iron, phosphorus
Asparagus	Asparagine, folic acid, potassium, phosphorus, riboflavin, vitamin C
Banana	Energy, fibre, folic acid, magnesium, potassium, vitamin A
Basil	Volatile oils: linalol, limonene, estragole
Beetroot	Beta-carotene, calcium, folic acid, iron, potassium, vitamins B_6 and C
Blackcurrants	Anti-inflammatory/cancer-fighting phytochemicals, carotenoids, vitamin C
Blueberries	Anti-bacterial/cancer-fighting phytochemicals, carotenoids, vitamin C
Broccoli	Cancer-fighting phytochemicals, folic acid, iron, potassium, riboflavin, vitamins A and C
Cabbage family	Cancer-fighting phytochemicals, folic acid, potassium, vitamins A, C and E
Carrots	Carotenoids, folic acid, magnesium, potassium, vitamin A
Celery	Coumarins, potassium, vitamin C
Chard (Swiss)	Calcium, cancer-fighting phytochemicals, carotenes, iron, phosphorus, vitamins A and C
Cherries	Cancer-fighting phytochemicals, flavonoids, magnesium, potassium, vit C
Chicory	Bitter, liver-stimulating terpenoids, folic acid, iron, potassium, vitamin A (if unblanched)
Chives	Beta-carotene, cancer-fighting phytochemicals, vitamin C
Cinnamon	Coumarins, tannins and volatile oils with mild, sedative/analgesic blood pressure-lowering effects
Cloves	Volatile oil (especially eugenol) with anti-nausea, antiseptic anti-bacterial and analgesic properties
Coriander	Coumarins, flavonoids, linalol
Cranberries	Cancer-fighting phytochemicals, specific urinary anti-bacterials, vitamin C
Cucumber	Folic acid, potassium, silica, small amounts of beta-carotene in the skin
Dates	Fibre, folic acid, fruit sugar, iron, potassium
Fennel	volatile oils: fenchone, anethole and anisic acid
Figs	Beta-carotene, cancer-fighting phytochemicals, fibre, ficin, iron, potassium

Garlic	Anti-bacterial and antifungal sulphur compounds, cancer and heart disease-fighting phytochemicals
Ginger	Circulatory-stimulating zingiberene and gingerols
Grapes	Natural sugars, powerful antioxidant flavonoids, vitamin C
Grapefruit	Beta-carotene, bioflavonoids – especially naringin, which thins the blood and lowers cholesterol, vitamin C
Jalapeño pepper	Carotenoids, capsaicin: a circulatory stimulant, flavonoids
Kiwi fruit	Beta-carotene, bioflavonoids, fibre, potassium, vitamin C
Lamb's lettuce	Folic acid, iron, potassium, vitamins A, C and B_6, zinc. Also contains calming phytochemicals
Leeks	Anti-arthritic, anti-inflammatory substances, cancer-fighting phytochemicals, folic acid, potassium, diuretic substances, vitamins A and C
Lemon	Bioflavonoids, limonene, potassium, vitamin C
Lettuce	Calcium, folic acid, phosphorus, potassium, sleep-inducing phytochemicals, vitamins A and C
Lime	Bioflavonoids, limonene, potassium, vitamin C
Mango	Beta-carotene, flavonoids, potassium, other antioxidants, vitamin C
Melon	Folic acid, potassium, small amounts of B vitamins, vitamins A and C
Milk	Calcium, protein, riboflavin, zinc
Mint	Antispasmodic volatile oils, flavonoids, menthol
Mixed salad leaves	Calcium, folic acid, phosphorus, potassium, sleep-inducing phytochemicals (darkest leaves contain the most nutrients), vitamins A and C
Molasses	Calcium, iron, magnesium, phosphorus
Nutmeg	Myristicin: mood enhancing and hallucinogenic in excess; phytochemicals that aid sleep and digestion
Oranges and other citrus fruits	Bioflavonoids, calcium, folic acid, iron, limonene, potassium, thiamine, vitamin B_6 and C
Parsley	Calcium, iron, potassium, vitamins A and C
Parsnip	B vitamins, folic acid, inulin, potassium, vitamin E
Passion-fruit	Beta-carotene, phytochemicals which are antiseptic, sedative and mildly laxative, vitamin C
Pawpaw	Beta-carotene, flavonoids, magnesium, papain: a digestive enzyme, vit C
Peaches	Beta-carotene, flavonoids, potassium, vitamin C
Peanuts	B vitamins, folic acid, protein, iron, zinc

Pears	Soluble fibre, vitamin C
Peppers	Beta-carotene, folic acid, potassium, phytochemicals that prevent blood clots, strokes and heart disease, vitamin C
Pineapple	Enzymes: especially bromelain, helpful for angina, arthritis and physical injury, vitamin C
Plums	Beta-carotene, malic acid: an effective aid to digestion, vitamins C and E
Pomegranate	Beta-carotene, enzymes with anti-diarrhoeal properties, heart-protective phytochemicals, vitamin E
Prunes	Beta-carotene, fibre, iron, niacin, potassium, vitamin B6
Pumpkin	Folic acid, potassium, small amounts of B vitamins, vitamins A and C
Purslane	Essential fatty acids and cleansing bitter alkaloids, folic acid, vits C and E
Radishes	Iron, magnesium, phytochemicals that stimulate gall bladder and heal mucous membranes, potassium, vitamin C
Rosemary	Flavonoids, volatile oils: borneol, camphor, limonene
Sage	Phenolic acids, phyto-oestrogens, thujone: an antiseptic
Sesame seeds	B vitamins, calcium, folic acid, magnesium, niacin, protein, vitamin E
Sorrel	Carotenoids, iron, protective phytochemicals, vitamin C
Soya milk	Calcium, phytoestrogens especially genistein: a powerful breast, ovarian and prostate cancer-fighter, protein. If fortied, also vitamin D
Spinach	Beta-carotene, cancer-fighting phytochemicals, chlorophyll, folic acid, iron, lutein, xeaxanthine
Spring greens	Beta-carotene, cancer-fighting phytochemicals, carotenoids, iron, vit C
Spring onion	Cancer-fighting phytochemicals, diuretic, anti-arthritic and anti-inflammatory substances, folic acid, potassium, vitamins A and C
Strawberries	Anti-arthritic phytochemicals, beta-carotene, vitamins C and E
Sweet potato	Beta-carotene and other carotenoids, cancer-fighting phytochemicals, protein, vitamins C and E
Thyme	Flavonoids, volatile oils: antiseptic thymol and carvol
Tomatoes	Beta-carotene, lycopene, potassium, vitamins C and E
Watercress	Anti-bacterial mustard oils, beta-carotene, iron, phenethyl isothiocyanate: specific lung cancer fighter for smokers, vitamins C and E
Watermelon	Folic acid, potassium, small amounts of B vitamins, vitamins A and C
Yoghurt: milk	Beneficial bacteria, calcium, protein, riboflavin, zinc
Yoghurt: soya	Calcium, phytoestrogens, especially genistein: a powerful breast, ovarian and prostate cancer fighter. If fortified, also contains vitamin D

index

Thanks to...

The publisher and author would like to thank all of the children who modelled for the photography, including Becky, Flynn, Livvy, Lucca, Millie, Rufus, Ted and Violet.

The publisher would also like to thank Proven Products Ltd for the loan of a Superjuicer for photography.